TANGRAM
PUZZLE FUN

Kid tested
by
RORY
BERGER
AGE 8

HIGHLIGHTS PRESS
HONESDALE, PENNSYLVANIA

MAKE A WHALE

SEA STUMPERS

The sea is a silly place! To solve these riddles, use the fractions of the words below to fill in the blanks.

What do you call a whale that talks a lot?

First 3/4 of BLUE
Middle 1/3 of BUBBLE
First 2/5 of ERASE
First 1/2 of MOON
Last 1/3 of YOU
Last 1/2 of WITH

A _ _ _ _ _ _ _ _ _
_ _ _ _ _ _

Why don't crabs share?

Middle 1/3 of FATHER
Last 2/5 of HONEY
First 2/3 of ART
First 1/4 of EDGE
Last 1/2 of DISH
First 2/3 of ELF
First 1/4 of LOOP
Last 1/2 of OF
First 1/3 of ISLAND
Last 1/5 of LUNCH

Because _ _ _ _ _ _ _ _
_ _ _ _ _ _ _ _ _ _ _

BONUS
Are there more green or blue fish in the scene?

MAKE A DOG

PUZZLING PUPS

Amanda, Noah, and Sophia are picking up their dogs from Top-Dog Training School. Using the clues below, can you match each dog with its age, its owner, and the trick it knows best?

Use the chart to keep track of your answers. Put an X in each box that can't be true and an O in boxes that match.

1. The oldest dog, Pawla, has learned to "heel" but still needs to work on "sit" and "come."

2. Noah's three-year-old dog is one year younger than Amanda's and one year older than Sophia's.

3. Wiggles always comes when called.

4. Rocket is two years old.

	WIGGLES	ROCKET	PAWLA
TWO YEARS OLD			
THREE YEARS OLD			
FOUR YEARS OLD			
AMANDA			
NOAH			
SOPHIA			
"HEEL"			
"SIT"			
"COME"			

Today's Lessons
"Heel," "Sit," and "Come"

I B K T
R E C T A

BONUS
Unscramble the single letters on the board to answer the riddle below.

What do you call a dog that designs doghouses?

A _ _ _ _ _ - _ _ _ _ _ _

5

MAKE A HOUSE

HOUSE HUNT

The geography club is having its first meeting at River's house. He gave the club members the following directions. Can you find his house?

1. I am south of B Street.

2. I live on a corner.

3. I am north of C Street.

4. There is a blue house directly north of my house.

BONUS

When River's friend Atlas heads home from River's house, he travels two houses east, two houses north, and then one house west. Which house is Atlas's?

MAKE A BIRD

BIRDWATCHING

There are 14 hidden birds in this scene. Can you find them all?

MAKE A LION

TOY-STORE TEASER

Each stuffed animal costs a different dollar amount. The totals for all four stuffed animals across each row and down each column are noted. Can you figure out the price of each type of stuffed animal?

HINT
The lion costs $6.00.

Row totals: $17, $28, $20, $26
Column totals: $24, $22, $23, $22

LION: _____

FROG: _____

BEAR: _____

PENGUIN: _____

MAKE A FISH

SEA SEARCH

Can you find the octopus hiding among the fish? Then find the
12 hidden seashells.

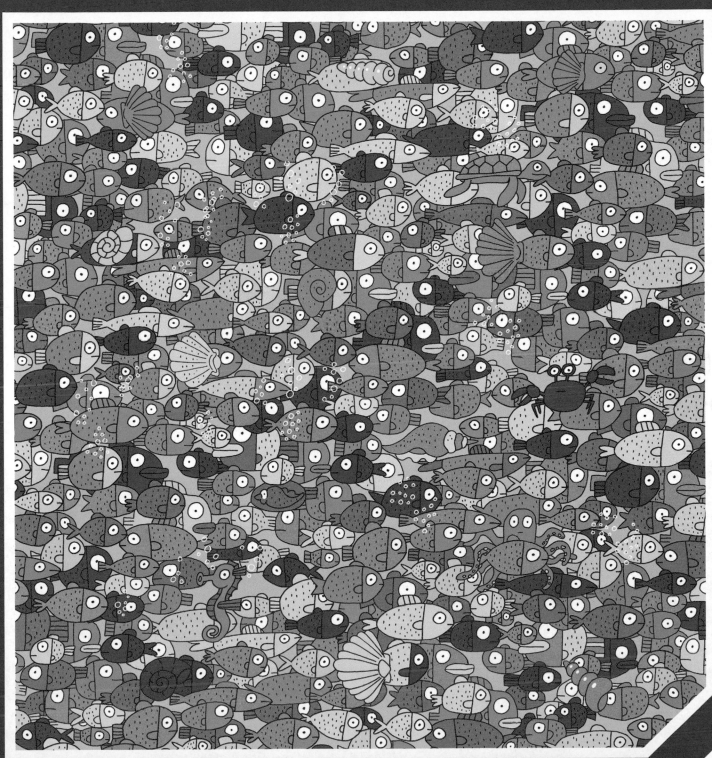

MAKE A ROSE

ROWS OF ROSES

Take some time to stop and smell the roses.
Which two columns contain the same six roses?

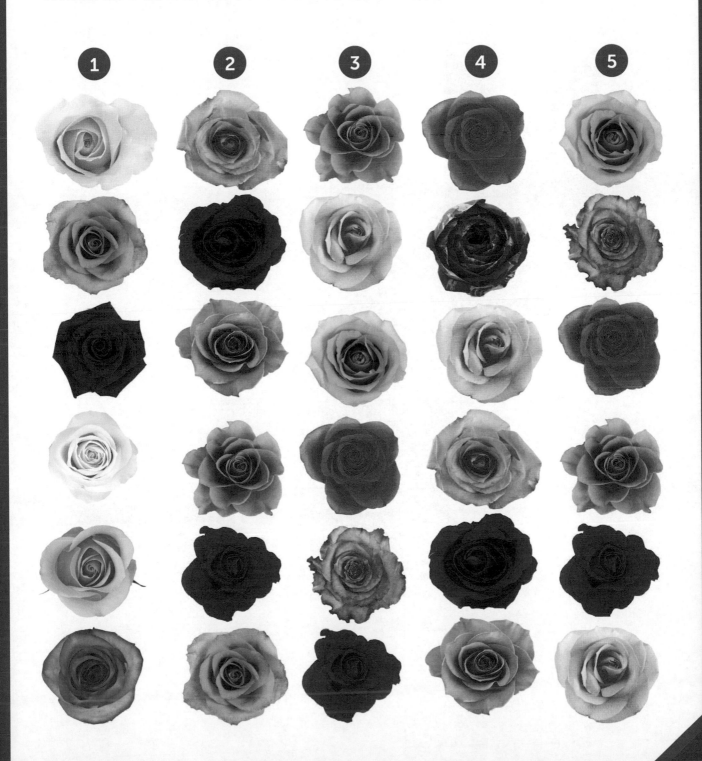

MAKE A CAT

CRAZY CATS

Follow the directions to cross out certain boxes. When you're done, write the remaining letters in order from left to right and top to bottom. They will give you the answer to the riddle.

Cross out all numbers divisible by 4.
Cross out all numbers divisible by 5.

M 8 (crossed out)	A 11	Y 40	N 24	N 17	A 12
O 19	M 16	C 23	E 20	C 15	A 30
L 32	I 25	F 4	T 31	O 10	O 34
R 45	P 18	D 5	R 55	X 28	Y 44
Z 35	E 20	U 38	B 65	T 25	W 52
S 22	K 36	N 48	H 50	N 60	S 26

What do you call a cat that has lost one of its nine lives?

__ __ __ __ __ __ __ - __ __ __ __

MAKE A SAILBOAT

TIC TAC BOAT

What do the boats in each row (horizontally, vertically, and diagonally) have in common?

Loopy Language

Can you match each language to its way of saying boat?

1. ___ German
2. ___ Spanish
3. ___ Welsh
4. ___ Indonesian
5. ___ Hmong
6. ___ Swahili
7. ___ French

A. mashua
B. perahu
C. le bateau
D. das Boot
E. cwch
F. el barco
G. nkoj

MAKE A RABBIT

PARTY PATH

Calvin has arrived at the location of his cousin's birthday party, but where is everyone? Help him get to the party by starting at the 9 in the top corner. You may move to a new box by adding 4 or subtracting 5. Move up, down, left, or right.

START

9	15	18	10	15	19
4	7	11	21	16	20
8	12	15	5	12	15
15	11	10	14	17	10
12	17	6	9	13	14
9	18	21	7	20	18

FINISH

21

MAKE A GIRAFFE

SKELETON DETECTION

Have you ever wondered what it would be like to wear X-ray glasses at the zoo? Unscramble the 10 animal names. Then match each animal to its skeleton.

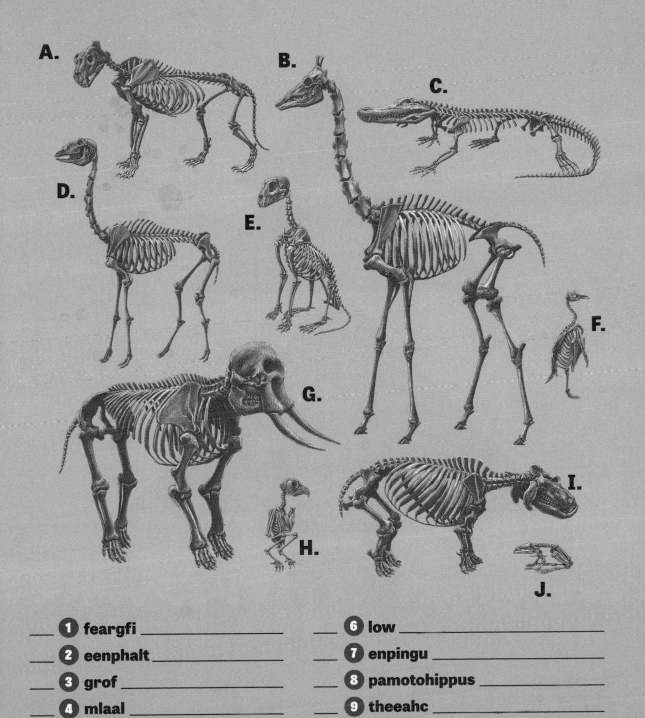

A.
B.
C.
D.
E.
F.
G.
H.
I.
J.

___ **1** feargfi _____

___ **2** eenphalt _____

___ **3** grof _____

___ **4** mlaal _____

___ **5** noli _____

___ **6** low _____

___ **7** enpingu _____

___ **8** pamotohippus _____

___ **9** theeahc _____

___ **10** raltogali _____

MAKE A TREE

TRICKY TRIANGLE TREES

Each tree has the numbers 1 through 6 running along the sides, and each of the sides add up to the number in the middle of the tree. Can you place the numbers so that everything adds up correctly?

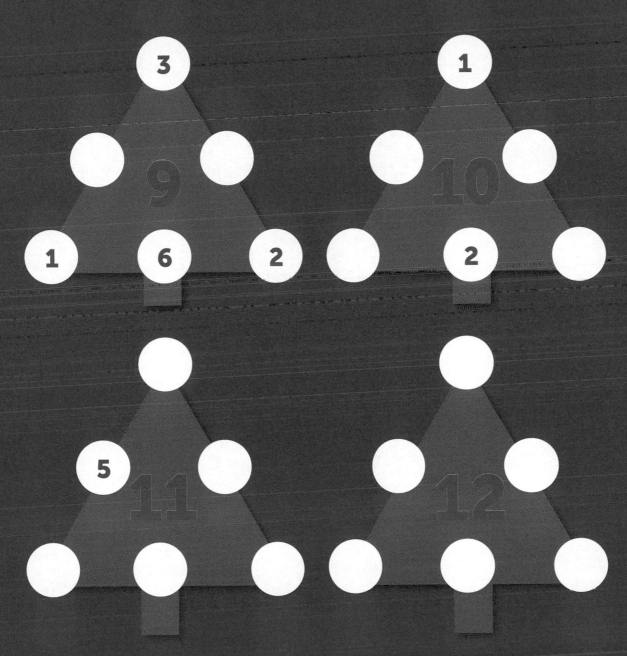

MAKE A ROCKET SHIP

ANSWERS

PAGE 2

PAGE 3
What do you call a whale that talks a lot?
A **BLUBBER MOUTH**

Why don't crabs share?
Because **THEY ARE SHELLFISH.**

BONUS!
There are more green fish.

PAGE 4

PAGE 5
WIGGLES
THREE YEARS OLD, NOAH, "COME"

ROCKET
TWO YEARS OLD, SOPHIA, "SIT"

PAWLA
FOUR YEARS OLD, AMANDA, "HEEL"

BONUS!
What do you call a dog that designs doghouses?
A BARK—ITECT

PAGE 6

PAGE 7
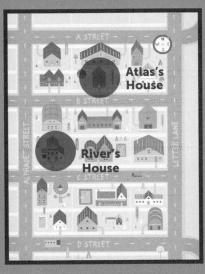

PAGE 8

PAGE 9

PAGE 10

ANSWERS

PAGE 11

LION: $6.00
FROG: $3.00
TEDDY BEAR: $5.00
PENGUIN: $8.00

PAGE 12

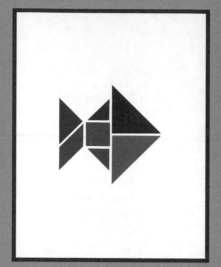

PAGE 13

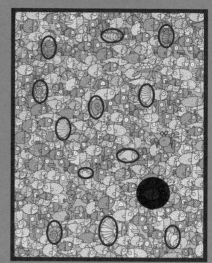

PAGE 14

PAGE 15

COLUMNS:
3 and 5

PAGE 16

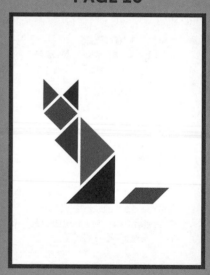

PAGE 17

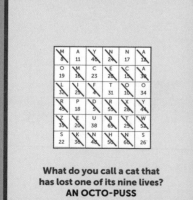

What do you call a cat that
has lost one of its nine lives?
AN OCTO-PUSS

PAGE 18

PAGE 19

Loopy Language
1. D (German: das Boot)
2. F (Spanish: el barco)
3. E (Welsh: cwch)
4. B (Indonesian: perahu)
5. G (Hmong: nkoj)
6. A (Swahili: mashua)
7. C (French: le bateau)

ANSWERS

31

PAGE 20

PAGE 21

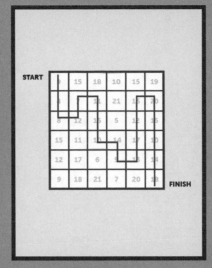

PAGE 22

PAGE 23

Skeleton Detection
1. giraffe (B)
2. elephant (G)
3. frog (J)
4. llama (D)
5. lion (A)
6. owl (H)
7. penguin (F)
8. hippopotamus (I)
9. cheetah (E)
10. alligator (C)

PAGE 24

PAGE 25

PAGE 26

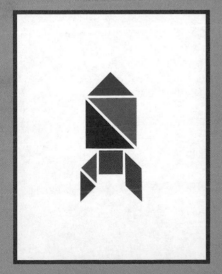

PAGE 27

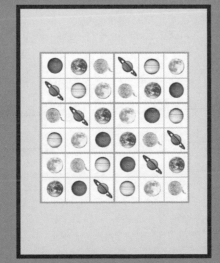

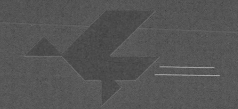

Russ Cox (11); Jack Desrocher (4, 16); Travis Foster (13); Kelly Kennedy (5); Dave Klug (9); Pat Lewis (3); Mike Moran (2, 6, 8, 10, 14, 18, 24); Shaw Nielsen (7); Eugenia Nobati (23); Sean Parkes (12); Robert Prince (19); Marta Ruliffson (25); Amanda Sobolak (20); Nuno Alexandre Vieira (21); Brian White (17); Jupiterimages Corporation (27); kaisphoto/GI (15); Liliboas/GI (15); Nikita Petrov/GI (2–3); Pacha M Vector/GI (12); Halyna Lakatosh/GI (22–23); kbeis/GI (26–27); Front cover image by Steven Wood

For information about permission to reprint selections from this book, please contact permissions@highlights.com.

Published by Highlights Press
815 Church Street
Honesdale, Pennsylvania 18431
ISBN: 978-1-63962-089-0
Manufactured in Dongguan, Guangdong, China
Mfg. 05/2023
First edition
Visit our website at Highlights.com.
10 9 8 7 6 5 4 3 2 1